Georgian Gardens

Georgian Gardens

Anne Jennings

ENGLISH HERITAGE

IN ASSOCIATION WITH THE MUSEUM OF GARDEN HISTORY

Front cover: **A view from the Cascade Terrace at Chiswick House, London,** *by George Lambert and William Hogarth*

Back cover: **The terrace at Wrest Park, Bedfordshire, with the orangery in the** *distance*

Published by English Heritage, 23 Savile Row, London W1S 2ET
in association with the Museum of Garden History, Lambeth Palace Road,
London SE1 7LB

First published 2005

ISBN 1 85074 904 3
Product code 50928

A CIP catalogue for this book is available from the British Library

Edited and brought to press by Adèle Campbell
Designed by Michael McMann
Technical editor Rowan Blaik
Printed by Bath Press

CONTENTS

Introduction

This book explores the origins of Georgian gardens. It looks at how they were designed and highlights the gradual move from formal 17th-century designs towards a 'natural' landscape style. Large or small, the gardens of the Georgian period were designed as places for relaxation and, equally importantly, they were used to demonstrate the owner's status and his understanding of taste and style.

Many eminent Georgian thinkers and writers, such as Pope and Walpole, were also keen amateur gardeners. Their work gives us an insight into how Georgians felt about their gardens and what influenced their tastes. Ideas brought home from the Grand Tour played a powerful part in shaping English gardens and cultural and artistic influence from continental Europe was significant. But the 18th century saw Britain staking its own claim on garden and landscape design and the English Landscape Movement remains internationally influential. The explosion of plant-hunting expeditions and the expansion of commercial nurseries are further testament to how rapidly the business of gardening grew during the 18th century.

Practical 'how-to' sections in the book provide tips on creating Georgian-style features in your own garden, and the lists of plants and trees available to 18th-century gardeners will help to evoke a Georgian feel. The availability of plants in UK nurseries is also given.

Cosmos bipinnatus *was introduced to Britain during the Georgian period*

The era commonly referred to as 'Georgian' covers just over a century, from 1715 to 1837. It begins with the reign of George I, includes the Regency period that ended in 1830 with the death of George IV, and concludes after the short subsequent reign of William IV, which lasted until Queen Victoria's accession in 1837. The 18th century is often referred to as a 'long century', in part because of the many social, economic and political changes that took place. In the Georgian period, perhaps more than at any other time, gardens directly reflected these cultural developments.

As the 18th century progressed, the Georgian upper and middle classes enjoyed increasing wealth and improved standards of education. Britain was becoming a significant international force and the foundations of the British Empire were being laid, thanks in part to the activities of the East India Company and its expanding trading territory. Maritime explorations helped ensure the nation's dominance of new territories; with, for example, Captain James Cook's circumnavigation of the globe in 1770, when he claimed New Zealand and Australia for the British crown. Imported goods had an huge impact on life in Britain – cotton, sugar, tobacco and tea all became increasingly available during this period. For the first time plants were arriving in Britain from all five continents and the number of plants cultivated in Britain saw a fivefold increase in the Georgian period, from 1,000 to 5,000.

> '...the retiring and again assembling shades...'

Wrest Park, Bedfordshire. Thomas Archer's pavilion seen across Long Water

More and more affluent young men were embarking on the 'Grand Tour' – extended trips to the Continent to learn about the culture, art and landscapes of other countries, particularly of ancient Greece and Italy. The dramatic landscapes they encountered were an inspiration to these travellers, who were moved to record their feelings and experiences in diaries and letters. Their descriptions of the terror, melancholy and elation they experienced on their journeys were to have a great influence on garden design in the following decades. Reactions and responses to the Grand Tour contributed towards a growing appreciation that landscapes were more than merely beautiful – they could also inspire emotion.

The orangery at Wrest Park, built in the 1830s

European culture had a great influence on British taste during much of the Georgian era. Classical Italian art and buildings, especially those designed by Andrea Palladio in the 16th century, continued to inspire the nation's architects who were to gradually integrate Italian ideas and style into British gardens and landscape features. Early 18th-century social commentators and writers Alexander Pope and Horace Walpole were among many intellectuals of the time who stimulated philosophical debate about art and culture, with landscapes playing a large part in discussions as well as featuring in their political and satirical writings. Walpole included a description of Pope's Strawberry Hill garden in his *On Modern Gardening*, written in 1780:

> *The passing through the gloom from the grotto to the opening day, the retiring and again assembling shades, the dusky groves, the larger lawn, and the solemnity of the termination at the cypresses that lead up to his mother's tomb, are managed with exquisite judgement.*

The middle and upper classes were deeply concerned with matters of taste and style, and literature, art and music were all important. Spa towns such as Bath and Harrogate became popular venues for balls, music recitals and readings. By the late 18th century, the romantic and idealistic work of poets

and writers such as William Wordsworth and William Blake, followed by that of Keats, Shelley and Byron, reflected the mood of the time. Contemporary fiction was increasingly popular too and Jane Austen's novels were enjoyed, as they are today, for their detailed observations of upper-middle-class Georgian life, society and gardens:

'Every time I come into this shrubbery I am
more struck with its growth and beauty. Three
years ago, this was nothing but a rough
hedgerow along the upper side of the field, never
thought of as anything, or capable of becoming
anything; and now it is converted into a walk,
and it would be difficult to say whether most
valuable as a convenience or an ornament...'

Jane Austen, *Mansfield Park*, 1814

The number of upper-middle-class gentlemen (the gentry)
was increasing; many made a great deal of money from wool,
cotton and mining during the Industrial Revolution and were
able to build large country houses with acres of land. The
party political system was controlled by the upper classes and
this ensured that the landed aristocracy became even more
powerful and influential. They were able to increase their land
holdings, often through the abuse of enclosure rights, and
create large gardens and designed landscapes that were
effective ways of demonstrating social status. Socialising in the
country was an important affair and large house parties
provided the opportunity to show off the latest gardens,
created by the most fashionable names in garden design and
landscape architecture.

Garden development – people and influences

The formal Renaissance-inspired gardens that had been fashionable throughout the 16th and 17th centuries remained popular during the early Georgian period. Some were beautifully recorded in *Britannia Illustrata*, which was produced by two Dutchmen in 1707. The combined skills of draughtsman Leonard Knyff (1650–1721) and engraver Johannes Kip (1653–1722) resulted in a series of invaluable pictorial records, with 'birds-eye' views of 80 English country houses and landscapes. Though the views were occasionally, and deliberately, idealised, they clearly demonstrate that strong French, Italian and Dutch influence remained in the first part of the 18th century, with long avenues of clipped trees, topiary, hedges, formal water features and elaborate parterres still very much in vogue.

A combination of factors caused a gradual change in tastes, however. The landed gentry were beginning to tire of formal gardens and resented the cost of maintaining elaborate hedges and intricate topiary, much of which was beginning to deteriorate with age. The formal styles popular for so long were being ousted by themes inspired by the Grand Tour and the horticultural aspirations of the Georgian country gentleman changed. He now wanted his garden to reflect the latest fashions and took inspiration from classical Roman art, literature and poetry. Perceptions about the natural world were changing too: nature was no longer something to be

'...we are tired, instead of being further entertained...'

Johannes Kip's birds-eye view of Coberly, London

feared, but could be tamed and even improved upon, and the
desire to enclose gardens with high walls and hedges declined.
A combination of these factors ensured a slow but steady
move towards loosening formality and integrating flowing lines
into garden and landscape design. The Georgian aristocracy
was ready to embrace the Landscape Movement.

Topiary at Squerryes Court, Kent. Early 18th-century gardens such as these were among the last to be laid out in a formal style

'...nor is there anything more shocking than a stiff, regular garden; where after we have seen one quarter thereof, the very same is repeated in all the remaining parts, so that we are tired, instead of being further entertained with something new as expected...'

Batty Langley, *New Principles of Gardening*, 1728

View across the south parterre and gardens of Wrest Park, Bedfordshire, laid out in the early 18th century

The Georgian gardener

Professional gardening was an attractive means of earning a living in the Georgian period, for educated and uneducated alike. Opportunities ranged from work as a 'jobbing' gardener to the enormously responsible position of head gardener, and in specialisms such as garden design and nursery work. On large country estates, garden staff received a similar scale of pay and conditions to house staff, but the head gardener was held in particularly high regard. He would have been an educated and articulate man, sometimes earning as much as £100 per year, and his responsibilities would have included overseeing a team of under gardeners, managing a budget and laying out new gardens. As well as a team of permanent under gardeners, unskilled labourers, including women, were employed on a seasonal basis, carrying out tasks like weeding or harvesting produce from the kitchen garden.

Gardening equipment was still relatively basic and relied on manual and horse power. Even the massive earth moving required for recontouring land and creating lakes was done by hand, with some horse-drawn agricultural machinery supplementing the efforts of the labourers. The motorised lawn mower was not introduced until 1830 and it was several years before a lighter, user-friendly model came into general use. In 1829, when William Cobbett referred to 'the mower' in *The English Gardener*, he was in fact referring to the gardener and his scythe:

During the month of May, grass must be mowed once a week. From the first of June, to the middle of July, and especially if the weather be wet, twice a week may be necessary... The mower can operate only in the dew; he must be at work by day-light, and the grass must be swept up before it be dry... A good short-grass mower is a really able-workman; and, if the plat have a good bottom; he will leave it very nearly as smooth and as even as the piece of green cloth which covers the table on which I am writing...

Above: The parterre gardener, 18th-century German engraving

Right and far right: Garden equipment from Sharp's 18th-century catalogue

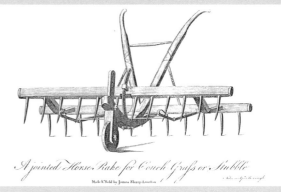

A jointed Horse Rake for Couch Grass or Stubble

Made & Sold by James Sharp London

Rather than being suddenly swept away by landscape gardens as is often assumed, formal gardens underwent a gradual metamorphosis that took almost 40 years. Even then, some ornate gardens survived into the later Georgian period, when the tide turned once more in favour of floral gardens.

Two important figures represent the transition between 17th-century formality and the more naturalistic 18th-century landscape designs. At a time when educated men were increasingly debating the meaning and interpretation of nature, writer and garden designer Stephen Switzer (1682–1745) developed the idea that the landscape surrounding a country house could be beautiful as well as functional. He drew inspiration from the geometry used in formal gardens and favoured straight lines in his designs for rides, walks and avenues of trees. But he also included the wider landscape in his work, to create vistas beyond the boundaries of the garden itself. Having worked at the famous Brompton Park Nursery in London, Switzer continued to be influenced by its owners, garden designers George London and Henry Wise.

Switzer gradually rejected extravagant formality, though he still used it immediately around the house. He referred to his own work as 'Forest Gardening' or 'Rural Gardening' and expanded on these theories in his 1718 book, *Ichnographia Rustica*, which

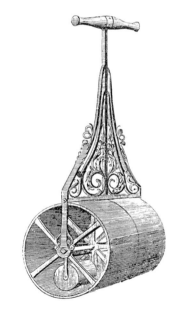

A Divided Garden Roller with Ballances

Made & Sold by James Sharp London

was originally published in 1715 as *Nobleman, Gentleman and Gardener's Recreation:*

> *Those large sums of money that have been*
> *buried within the narrow limits of a high wall*
> *upon the trifling and diminutive beauties of*
> *greens and flowers would be employed to better*
> *advantage lightly spread over great parks and*
> *forests.*

Another influential character, and one who was to have even greater impact than Switzer during this transition period, was Charles Bridgeman (1690–1738). Like Switzer, Bridgeman had worked at the Brompton Nursery and, with Henry Wise, became Royal Gardener to George I. Under George II he carried out large landscaping works and extensive tree-planting at Richmond and later worked there with William Kent, as well as at Stowe in Buckinghamshire. He had gradually moved away from formal garden designs to working with the broader landscape, introducing woodland walks and lakes. Bridgeman effectively prepared the way for the more dramatic style of Lancelot 'Capability' Brown, and one of his most important landscape devices, the 'ha-ha', was adopted and used extensively by Brown. The ha-ha developed from a military idea, and was a grass-covered ditch or sunken wall that imperceptibly separated the landscape near the house

The ha-ha remained a popular device, as shown by this design illustrated in Thomas Mawson's The Art and Craft of Garden Making, *1900*

from that beyond. This clever feature kept livestock at a distance while allowing an uninterrupted view of the whole landscaped garden. Bridgeman enjoyed large-scale projects and experimented with earth-moving to create new contours and levels, such as the dramatic grass amphitheatre that can still be seen at Claremont in Surrey.

Bridgeman shared with his friend, the poet Alexander Pope, an appreciation of the *genius loci*, or what he referred to as 'the genius of the place'. This was a philosophy that became increasingly important during the development of the English

Landscape Movement and encouraged designers and landscapers to recognise and respond to the natural characteristics of a site.

Early design for Ring Hill Temple at Audley End, Essex, by Robert Adam, reflecting the 'Augustan' style

Pope's literary work, and indeed his own garden at Twickenham, took inspiration from classical Rome, where landscapes provided the setting for philosophical discussion and reflection. Ornaments, statuary and seats were strategically placed to help stimulate debate. This style, sometimes referred to as 'Augustan', influenced Bridgeman's work for Lord Burlington at Chiswick House in the 1720s.

An early-18th-century view of the gardens at Chiswick House, London, by Pieter Rysbrack

Pope's garden included an elaborate grotto decorated with coloured stones and gems, inspired by the richly decorated caves and grottoes of ancient Italy. These were a popular addition to the 18th-century garden and another was made at Chatsworth House in Derbyshire for the wife of the 5th Duke of Devonshire, who loved crystals and gems. Others can still be seen at Stourhead in Wiltshire, Stowe in Buckinghamshire and Painshill in Surrey. Such features, together with hermitages, rustic structures and thatched buildings, were used increasingly over the following decades, as the natural materials and rural or humble associations were thought appropriate for the landscape garden setting. When the buildings were used as summerhouses or shelters, decorative floors were often laid with herringbone brick or mosaics of different materials. Thomas Wright of Durham (1711–86) was one of several designers who produced pattern books and catalogues for such rustic buildings.

Left and above: **The rustic bath house at Wrest Park, Bedfordshire, built in the 1770s. The floor is inlaid with pebbles and animal knuckle bones**

lay a mosaic floor

The Grand Tour was partly responsible for the popularity of mosaic paving in British gardens, as returning travellers described elaborate pavements and terraces they had seen in Italy. Thomas Wright, the Georgian rustic designer, recommended mosaics for the floors of summerhouses. Several natural materials were used, including horses' teeth and cleaned animal knuckles, but flint, tiles, bricks and pebbles were also used.

To make a mosaic in your garden you will need to find suitable materials; a range of pebbles, stones and slate can be bought in builders' yards or from landscape suppliers. It is fun to try and salvage materials yourself such as old bricks, roof tiles and, depending on where you live, flints or stones direct from your garden – remember it is illegal to collect large quantities of these materials from natural environments such as beaches. Relatively flat stones and large pebbles are best – the same shape you would use to skim across water.

3 inches 76 mm
4 inches 102 mm

Sand and Cement mix

hardcore

The following instructions are for a pebble mosaic, using smooth, oval stones. For other materials, such as brick, depths may need adjusting.

First, design a pattern for your mosaic. Start off with a simple geometric shape like a cross or a grid pattern. If your design is simple a basic sketch drawing will suffice, but more complex patterns should be drawn to scale. Think about incorporating a 'frame' of some kind, for example three rows of the same type of pebbles.

Dig out the area for the mosaic to a depth of c 200mm (8"). Unless the mosaic is positioned within well-established turf or an area of paving, the edges will need to be supported with a small concrete foundation and haunching (a sloping concrete shoulder).

Fill the excavated area with strongly compacted hardcore to a depth of 102mm (4") to provide a firm base suitable for walking on. (If your mosaic is in an area used by vehicles, deeper foundations will be required.)

Next, fill the remaining area with a mix of 1 part sharp sand, 1 part builder's sand, 1 part cement and 3 parts 5mm-grit/shingle, to a depth of approximately 76mm (3"). Gently firm this material but do not compact it.

Use string to ensure the lines of your pattern remain straight, and begin by pressing into place the frame, if you are using one, pushing the stones firmly down into the sand and cement mix so that the top surface lies level with the surrounding turf or paving.

Continue setting in the remaining pebbles until your pattern is complete, then gently spray the whole mosaic with water and leave to dry.

When the pebbles are dry, gently brush in a final dressing of the sand and cement mix, to roughly 5mm (1/4") from the top surface of the pebbles. Lightly sprinkle with water then cover with polythene and leave to dry.

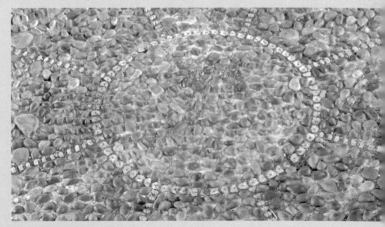

Detail of the floor of the bath house at Wrest Park

William Kent

William Kent (1685–1748) was one of a growing number of designers who practised a more informal approach to landscape design. Art and literature were becoming increasingly influential in the lives of wealthy and educated Georgians, and the popularity of paintings of the countryside around ancient Rome was inspiring designers to recreate similar scenes in the British landscape. The most famous practitioner was the architect, artist and designer William Kent whose work moved even closer than Bridgeman's to the landscape garden that Brown would eventually develop. Kent shared with Pope the view that 'all gardening is landscape painting', a philosophy that epitomised the style referred to as English Landscape School.

William Kent

Kent had studied art in Italy and one of his patrons was the influential supporter of the arts, Lord Burlington. Burlington's home at Chiswick House was inspired by the Italian Renaissance architect Palladio, who stressed the importance of relating buildings and architectural features to the landscape. When Kent joined Bridgeman at Chiswick, in 1733, they gradually softened the more formal lines of some of Bridgeman's earlier work. Kent never professed to be a gardener, but his artistic and architectural skills gave him an understanding of shape and form, and his large-scale planting schemes successfully complemented the overall landscape designs. At Rousham, Oxfordshire, Kent's experience in theatre design can be seen in the carefully-planned walks and striking architectural features like the Arcade and Pyramid. Horace Walpole celebrated Kent's approach to the landscape in his 1780 *Essays on Modern Gardening*:

> '…*At that moment appeared Kent, painter enough to taste the charms of landscape, bold and opinionated enough to dare and dictate, and born with a genius to strike out a great system from the twilight of imperfect essays. He leap'd the fence and saw that all nature was a garden…*'

The Temple of Concord in the grounds of Audley End, Essex, surrounded by a well-disguised ha-ha

Classical Italian art and the Renaissance clearly influenced Kent's work but his interpretation of it was dramatically different from those of the 17th century. His designs relied to a certain extent on a formal underlying structure, but he used flowing instead of straight lines and substituted regimented rows of clipped, evergreen topiary with graceful avenues of elm or horse chestnut.

Another popular way of integrating the wider landscape into the was the *ferme ornée* or 'ornamented farm'. Inspiration came from the 17th-century idea, later developed by Switzer, that a rural landscape could be beautiful and functional, hence a working farm and grazing animals were included as an element of the landscape design. *Fermes ornées* were created by Philip Southcote (1698–1788) at Woburn Farm in Surrey in the 1730s and by the poet, farmer, and landscape theorist William Shenstone (1714–63) at The Leasowes in Warwickshire. These concepts were not universally embraced, however, and as theories about the English landscape developed through the 18th century a later practitioner, Humphry Repton, criticised Shenstone for 'attempting to unite two objects so incompatible as ornament and profit'.

By the middle of the 18th century sophisticated debates about garden and landscape design had helped to accelerate the movement for change from the formal to the natural.

The 'halfway house' styles popularised by Bridgeman and Kent were radically redeveloped into the flowing lines and 'natural' scenes of the English landscape park, championed by the legendary Lancelot 'Capability' Brown.

William Tomkins's view of **Audley End and the Ring Temple,** *shows the influence of the ferme ornée*

The Georgian garden owner had a huge variety of styles, materials and manufacturers to choose from when it came to furnishing his garden.

William Kent took his inspiration from ancient Rome and his garden seats were ideal for the classically inspired temples, grottoes and arcades that graced the more formal, landscaped garden areas. These features were located with great care; they acted as 'eye-catchers' themselves but they also encouraged the walker to stop and admire a carefully constructed view (as well as affording rest and shelter).

Twickenham brothers Batty and Thomas Langley were highly influential in early 18th-century garden design. They popularised rustic and 'grotesque' furniture, carved and painted to imitate the boughs of trees (although items made from the real thing were even better), that was ideal for the wilder part of the garden. Rustic was one of many influences that were popular over the course of the Georgian period; Chinese motifs were popular too and there was a vogue for all things Alpine that found expression in thatched garden houses, for example.

Wrought iron lent itself well to garden seating and designers produced a range of chairs, benches and tables, often featuring 'woven' iron slats. With the advent of cast iron in the mid-18th century these elegant, hand-crafted designs could be mass produced. Highly ornamental iron garden buildings and seats were extremely popular in the Regency period, when the fashion for conservatories and french windows meant the garden was even more visible from the house. Perhaps most popular of all were the ornate canopied seats and tents that were *de rigeur* for outdoor entertaining. J B Papworth was foremost in the design of these elaborate features, for which he created canopies of canvas as well as copper- and iron-sheet; features that were soon adopted for the covered balconies and verandahs that became a hallmark of Regency architecture.

Two of Papworth's designs for ornate covered garden seats, from Ackermann's 1822 Repository of Arts

Lancelot 'Capability' Brown

Northumbrian-born Lancelot Brown (1716–83) was an educated man whose early talent for gardening, design and landscaping quickly developed into a highly profitable career. He eventually added architectural skills to his portfolio too. Brown gained his nickname from his habit of describing landscapes as having the 'capability' for improvement. His inspiration came not from classical Italy or experiences on the Grand Tour, nor from a love of painting or classical literature, but from a visionary passion to create landscapes that were, in his opinion, characteristically English.

Brown oversaw the development of the landscape at Stowe from 1741 to 1750, making changes to the earlier work of Bridgeman and Kent but working alongside Kent, who was still employed as a consultant on the estate. After Stowe, Brown went on to work for many wealthy clients and in 1764 was appointed Master Gardener at Hampton Court. For almost 40 years, Brown designed, constructed and managed the development of some of Britain's finest landscape parks, and had a virtual monopoly on landscape design. His work can be appreciated in its mature beauty today.

Brown's work is often referred to as the 'Serpentine' style, with sweeping lawns coming right up to the house, sinuous lakes, wide belts of trees and circular or curved driveways.

'Capability' Brown painted by Richard Cosway in the 1770s

Unlike Kent, he incorporated few classical features into his landscapes, preferring an occasional temple or bridge as a focal point rather than using a proliferation of statues and urns to evoke a classical feel. He is best known for his ambitious earth-moving works: widening rivers, damming streams, excavating enormous lakes and exaggerating or completely changing natural contours. A particularly good example of this large-scale landscaping can be seen at Blenheim Palace in Oxfordshire. In the days before heavy machinery it was no small task to execute these grand schemes.

Brown made a dramatic move away from earlier ideas that combined beauty with overt practicality in the landscape. He deliberately screened or disguised any utilitarian aspects of rural life, using trees and shelter belts to hide arable fields, farm buildings and kitchen gardens. A ha-ha or ditch ensured that the picturesque grazing animals did not interfere with the finely-scythed lawns near the house. Nevertheless, these landscape parks were on valuable agricultural land and the owner would have been reluctant to see his income reduced, so much of the 'view' was put to use: pasture was rented out, trees cut for timber, and dense woodlands used for game hunting. Man-made lakes were fished as stocks multiplied.

Capability Brown provided a complete service to his clients, staying personally involved from the first consultation and site visit, through the survey, design and construction, managing the projects and preparing detailed drawings throughout. Brown a popular man, well-liked by his clients, some of whom he worked with for many years, and he completed over 200 commissions in his 30-year career. His commitment and passion made him a wealthy man and his work, though often maligned both in his day and ours, is still considered by many to typify the beauty of a 'natural' English landscape.

> *Such was the effect of his genius that he will be least remembered. So closely did he copy Nature that his works will be mistaken for it.*
>
> Horace Walpole

Farming on the lower slopes of the garden at early 19th-century Norwood House, Surrey

Sublime, Picturesque and Gardenesque

By the late 18th century, discussions about landscape design were becoming increasingly philosophical. Heated arguments developed about the interpretation of nature and whether irregularity or geometry should be applied to the landscape. Rational argument suggested that science and mathematics alone could dictate beauty, for if this was not the case, how could beauty be measured? The counter view favoured a subjective interpretation of beauty, defined by observation and opinion.

The beauty of the wild landscapes of the Lake District, the Scottish Highlands and the European Alps, familiar to many through the Grand Tour, inspired the theory of the 'Sublime'. The emotive qualities of landscapes inspired debate and challenged designers to look beyond the merely aesthetic. Another school of thought favoured the concept of the 'Pictureseque', applying the term to any scene that would be suitable for painting or that looked as though it were part of a picture. Dramatic and rugged landscapes were particularly favoured. To help assess a landscape's potential as a Picturesque scene, a small frame called a Claude glass would be used to 'enclose' a section of a view. Some of the paintings of Gainsborough and Constable reflect Picturesque ideals. The ideas of clergyman William Gilpin were highly influential in the development of the Picturesque, particularly his *Books of Tours* of Wales and the Lake District. Landowner Sir Uvedale Price wrote at length on the differences

'...*in works of ART every trick ought to be avoided.*'

The Arum lily, Zantedeschia aethiopica, *introduced from South Africa in the 1730s*

between the Sublime and the Picturesque, arguing, for example, that uniformity was an essential element of the former, while the latter relied on variety.

To make things even more complicated, horticulturalist and garden writer John Claudius Loudon (1783–1843), who was to be an enormous influence on early and mid-Victorian gardening, invented the term 'Gardenesque'. By the end of the Georgian period he was using this term to describe a landscape that was designed to reflect art, rather than to imitate nature. Trees and shrubs were often planted as individual specimens rather than in more natural-looking groups or shrubberies, and he favoured the use of non-native species. Loudon argued that no form of gardening was natural and it was therefore inappropriate to attempt to recreate nature. By positioning plants in this way Loudon believed they could be appreciated for their individual beauty and interest.

'…if foreign trees and shrubs only are used, they may be planted in irregular masses or groups, and as single trees. If indigenous trees and shrubs are at any time introduced in the modern style of landscape-gardening, the greatest care should be taken not to crowd, or even group, them together in such a manner that a stranger might conclude they had grown up there naturally…'

John Loudon, *The Suburban Gardener and Villa Companion*, 1838

Debates about the landscape and how it should be portrayed and described grew increasingly intense, and complex issues surrounding the Picturesque still inspire debate among academics and artists today. When Uvedale Price published *Essays on the Picturesque* at the end of the 18th century, a furious disagreement ensued, with Price and the author Richard Payne Knight criticising 'Capability' Brown's landscapes for being too smooth, and lacking both the essential rugged appeal of the Sublime, and the artistic emphasis of the Picturesque. Price favoured more formality around the house with a landscaped park beyond, while allowing a wilderness to develop at the extremes of the site.

Humphry Repton

Humphry Repton (1752–1818) was a water-colourist and he combined this skill with his knowledge of gardening and architecture to offer a unique service to his clients. He prepared individually commissioned portfolios that became known as 'Red Books' because of their red-leather bindings.

The Red Books were a clever marketing tool unique to Repton; in them he illustrated his clients' gardens 'before' and 'after' recommended works took place, often using a system of delicate overlays to emphasise the dramatic changes that would unfold. Repton himself rarely supervised his projects,

Panoramic 'before' and 'after' views from Repton's Red Book for Antony House, Cornwall, c 1812

preferring to employ a clerk of works who would refer to the client's Red Book as the landscape took shape. Unlike Capability Brown he did not become rich through his work, but he offered an equally time-consuming service and was highly influential in and beyond the late Georgian period.

Humphry Repton's artistic background had a strong influence on his ideas about gardens and he declared that they should be 'works of art, rather than of nature'; this was a philosophy that John Claudius Loudon later expanded on in his theories of the Gardenesque. Repton's *Observations on the Theory and Practice of Landscape Gardening*, published in 1803, included a

list of 'objections' to the natural landscapes that were the hallmark of his famous predecessor, Capability Brown. Objection No. 9 was that:

> *Deception may be allowable in imitating the works of NATURE; thus artificial rivers, lakes and rock scenery, can only be great by deception, and the mind acquiesces in the fraud after it has been detected; but in works of ART every trick ought to be avoided. Sham churches, sham ruins, sham bridges, and everything that appears what it is not, disgusts when the trick is discovered.*

Repton had clear ideas on the position and content of the flower garden, which he believed 'should be detached and distinct from the general scenery of the place [and] rare plants of every description should be encouraged.' Fashion still dictated that the landscape near the house was laid out in a clean and simple style, and Repton recommended that '…except where it is annexed to the house, [the flower garden] should not be visible from the roads or general walks about the place. It may therefore be of a character totally different from the rest of the scenery, and its decorations should be as much those of art as of nature'. He gave instructions on preparing the ground for different types of plant, including American bog and aquatic species, and encouraged that 'above all there should be poles or hoops for those kind of creeping plants which spontaneously form themselves into graceful festoons, when encouraged and supported by art'.

Repton's *Observations* is a good indication that interest in plants was growing among late-18th-century garden owners, more so than in previous decades. The increasing availability of new, exotic specimens fuelled an appetite that would be insatiable for the next two centuries. At the same time,

37

Uvedale Price's ideas about anchoring the house within a more formal setting were becoming fashionable. Repton responded to this by designing terraces, balustrades and conservatories filled with ornamental plants. He incorporated island beds in the lawn near the house and created wide, sweeping lawns that led to a serpentine landscape, resulting in a gradual transition from the formality and ornamental planting near the house to the more natural scene beyond. He advocated a 'mixed garden' that incorporated a variety of different styles, an example of which can be seen at Ashridge in Hertfordshire, where an Italian garden, a rose garden, a grotto and an arboretum were incorporated into the landscape.

Though Repton was never a 'hands-on' landscape gardener in the style of Capability Brown, he was a first-class salesman and his Red-Book approach was an extremely effective marketing tool. The Red Books that survive today are invaluable records of the gardens he worked on. In the same way that Charles Bridgeman's work embodied the transition from the formal gardens of the 17th century to the landscape gardens of the 18th, Humphry Repton combined the Georgian love of natural landscapes with a return to popularity of ornamental planting; a trend that evolved into the Victorian flower garden.

create island beds

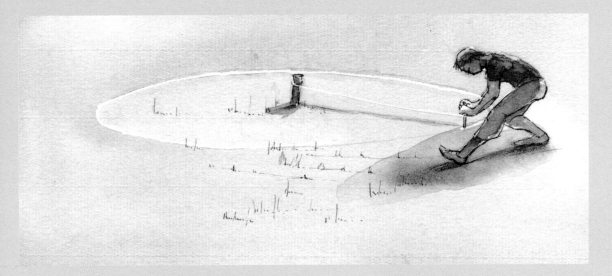

Island beds were popular in both town and country gardens by the late 18th-century. They were positioned within an area of lawn and were often circular, but sometimes had more organic, irregular shapes. The planting in an island bed was graded in height so that the tallest plants were at the centre and the lowest ones were at the front.

To make a circular island bed, measure some garden string to the radius of the circle you want to create. Attach the string to a wooden peg or garden cane and drive the cane into the turf where you want the centre of the bed to be. Pull the string taut then slowly mark out the circle by dragging a trowel or other sharp tool into the turf. If you prefer you can mark the outline by trickling sand in a line around the edge of the circle.

Remove the turf within the circle using a spade (you can get a special turf spade for this purpose though an ordinary garden spade will do). Dig the soil to a spade depth and incorporate some organic matter to improve its condition, and some bonemeal, chicken manure or general fertiliser as a nutrient feed. Lightly tread and level the soil. It is now ready for planting.

create island beds

Plants for '18th-century' island beds:

Tall plants

Cephalaria gigantea

Chelone glabra

Delphinium grandiflorum

Eryngium giganteum

Galega orientalis

Phlox paniculata

Verbascum phoenicium

Verbena bonariensis

Medium plants

Achillea filipendulina

Fuchsia magellanica

Gypsophila paniculata

Paeonia suffruticosa

Penstemon barbatus

Reseda odorata

Rosa damascena

Rosa rubiginosa

Small plants

Bergenia cordifolia

Dianthus alpinus

Geranium endressii

Hosta sieboldii

Nepeta racemosa syn mussinii

Stachys byzantina syn lanata

Viola odorata var flore pleno

Remember to select tall plants for the centre, then grade down in height until you are using low-growing specimens at the front. Depending on the size of your island bed, you could include shrubs for additional interest, or perhaps a rustic plant support in the middle for roses. Taller plants may need staking.

Above: Repton's ornamental planting remained popular into the 20th century – this photograph was taken in 1905

Left: Perennial phlox, Phlox paniculata

Urban gardens

An elegant, well-designed garden was not the sole preserve of the country landowner but was equally important to those who spent part or all of their time in town. Nurseryman Thomas Fairchild wrote in his book *The City Gardener* in 1722 that 'almost every Body, whose Business requires them to be constantly in Town, will have something of a Garden…'. As the urban population increased towards the end of the Georgian period there was a boom in house-building and John Loudon produced a series of designs for small town gardens in *Hints on the Formation of Gardens and Pleasure Grounds* published in 1812.

Urban gardens came in various sizes. Those near the town centre were smaller than those further out, and the gardens of terraced houses were narrower than those of the detached or semi-detached villa. Front gardens or forecourts tended to be small and were laid out in a very simple manner, sometimes with a central lawn and perimeter borders planted with a hedge or shrubs. Window boxes and pots on balconies were popular at both the front and back of the house.

The main gardening activity took place to the rear of the house and the layout and design often reflected personal tastes and ideas, much as it does today. Some householders, however, employed professional designers and architects who attempted to respond to the *genius loci* despite the obvious

'*…almost every Body…in Town, will have something of a Garden…*'

Argentinean vervain, Verbena bonariensis, *was introduced to Britain from South America in 1726*

The most fashionable aspired to the latest in garden design whatever the location; this Thames-side villa, drawn in 1775, belonged to the actor David Garrick

constraints of the town garden. This generally meant that the design would complement the architecture and style of the house, but it would also attempt to disguise or enhance the view beyond the boundary walls. At the edge of town, where houses were closer to the countryside, designers adopted William Kent's technique of 'borrowing' features from the wider landscape, such as churches or mills, to give the impression that the garden extended far into the distance.

Gardeners attend to the back garden at St James's Square, Bristol (Thomas Pole, early 19th century)

Restricted size and inflexible boundaries tended to dictate that small Georgian town gardens were formally laid out and, as a result, 17th-century influence lingered for longer in urban areas. Formal grass or box-edged parterres and gravel paths are clearly shown on plans and drawings of the period, although in larger gardens there were attempts to include more fashionable 18th-century elements, such as groves of shrubberies, glades and 'wilderness areas'.

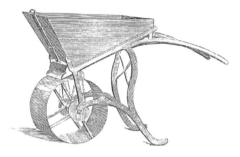

What the town gardener lacked in space he could make up for in growing a range of new and exotic plants in pots or window boxes. Wealthier people built fashionable conservatories that protected tender plants from the pollution and poor air of the city. Garden plants often failed to thrive in these urban environments and, in extreme cases, a

garden might have to be rejuvenated every year with new turf and fresh plants. It was not uncommon for pot-grown specimens to be plunged into the soil, to fill out a display or replace a dying plant.

Bath Georgian Garden

Henderson pinxt.   *Ward sculpt.*

The Dragon Arum.

London, Published by Dr. Thornton Decr. 1. 1801.

Plants

The 17th century had seen the establishment of various florists' societies and many of these thrived throughout the Georgian period. As interest in plants increased further towards the end of the 18th century, these societies focused on breeding specific species like auriculas, carnations and tulips with the aim of producing perfect flowers, purely for their aesthetic value.

It was an exciting time for new plant introductions, and orangeries and conservatories were filled with exotic plants that were brought into the main house when in bloom. Non-native trees and flowering shrubs grew in the garden, and were even planted in the landscape parks. By the end of the 18th century, gardeners and garden owners were once more becoming passionate plant collectors. The wealthy sought out new introductions and unknown plant varieties for both the garden and conservatory, and many educated people studied botany simply for pleasure. One of these, Dr John Fothergill (1712–80), was a medical doctor with a love of plants and an impressive botanical knowledge. His immense greenhouse at Upton House, West Ham (now West Ham Park), was full of plants gathered from all over the world and he was a great patron and financial supporter of the plant-hunting industry.

One of the first gardening magazines, *The Botanical Magazine*, appeared in 1787. It was founded by the botanist William

The Dragon Arum or Voodoo Lily, Arum maculatum *or* Dracunculus vulgaris, *from R J Thornton's* The Temple of Flora, *first published c 1800*

Curtis who had previously published *Flora Londinesis*, recording the wild flowers that grew within a 10-mile radius of London. The magazine proved far more popular than the book, appealing to wealthy garden owners who craved information about new and exotic plants. It was illustrated with fine botanical drawings by the best artists of the day, including James Sowerby. It continued to be published after Curtis's death, eventually merging in 1984 with *Kew Magazine*, which is still available today.

The Royal Botanic Gardens at Kew began in a modest way in 1759 but once Sir Joseph Banks was appointed director in 1771 it became an increasingly important force in the international movement and exchange of plants. Banks had

William Curtis's botanic gardens on Lambeth Marsh, painted by James Sowerby

accompanied Captain James Cook on his circumnavigation of the world, during which Cook discovered Australia, and had supervised the transportation of Antipodean plants to Britain.

Banks took every opportunity to arrange the transportation of botanical specimens to Kew and often persuaded the

captains of merchant ships to carry plants and seeds from foreign botanical collections. In his enthusiasm he even enroled a ship's surgeon, Archibald Menzies, to collect plants on his trip to Chile, with the result that the first Monkey Puzzle tree seedlings arrived at Kew in 1795. Gardener Francis Masson (1741–1806) was the first collector to be sent from Kew to South Africa, in 1772, from where he was to introduce pelargoniums, mesembryanthemums, ixias, gladioli and proteas. He introduced the cyad, *Encephalartos altensteinii*, which still thrives in Kew's Palm. From Kew, plants went on to other botanical collections and eventually became available to private garden owners. This international movement of plants also played an important role in meeting the demands of the growing British Empire, as it became necessary to transport food and raw materials between countries. For example, Captain William Bligh was commissioned to transport breadfruit from Tahiti to the West Indies to feed slaves. This voyage, on the *Bounty*, was to become infamous for the mutiny that left Bligh adrift on the pacific.

Banks gave specific instructions to his collectors, encouraging them to record information about local uses and natural habitats of their specimens, and when the hot houses at Kew became full he told them to concentrate on plants that would be hardy in Britain. William Hooker (1785–1865) took over the directorship of Kew on Banks's death in 1820 and continued his work of making Kew the finest botanic garden in the British Empire.

The Chelsea Physic Garden, founded in 1673, appointed perhaps its most influential Gardener in the 18th century: Philip Miller (1691–1771) had wide-ranging horticultural and botanical knowledge. He advised many important figures of the day about their plants and gardens and sent the first

Japanese wisteria, Wisteria floribunda

cotton seed to Georgia in 1733 and was a much-envied recipient of plants and seeds from the Philadelphian botanist John Bartram. During his 48 years' service, Miller developed the wide range of plants grown at the Physic Gardens today. He also wrote *The Gardener's Dictionary*, one of the most important botanical encyclopaedias of its times, which was published between 1731 and 1768. In 1770 Miller was replaced as Gardener by one of his former pupils, William Forsyth, after whom the plant *Forsythia* is named.

The final version of Miller's *Dictionary* used the new naming system of plants designed by the Swedish botanist Carl Linnaeus, which was first published in Linnaeus's *Systema Naturae* in 1735. His classification, based on the arrangement of the sexual parts of plants, reorganised the whole basis upon which plants were named, and simplified what had become a chaotic and complex system of classification. His theory produced the binomial classification grouping plants by genus and species, that is still used today.

The English Gardener, by countryman and politician William Cobbett, is a delightful book that is available as a reprinted edition today. It was written for the owners of large country houses and relates in particular to kitchen gardens, giving advice on the cultivation of ornamental and edible plants. It also provides a wealth of information about gardening

practice in the late 18th and early 19th centuries, and demonstrates how important kitchen gardens were in providing food for the house. The range of fruit and vegetables grown included apricots, cherries, apples, figs, mulberry, quince, nectarines, pears, potatoes, asparagus, melon, broccoli and cauliflower.

Increasing activity and interest in gardening encouraged a group of seven men to meet at Hatchards bookshop in Piccadilly in 1804, with the aim of founding an organisation for 'the improvement of horticulture'. Among them were Sir Joseph Banks, John Wedgewood, son of the potter Josiah, and

William Forsyth. After 20 years the fledgling Horticultural Society of London (later the Royal Horticultural Society) had 1,500 Fellows. In 1821 land at Chiswick was leased from the 6th Duke of Devonshire to create demonstration gardens, and over the following 25 years the Society sent plant hunters to China, Africa and North and South America. Among these was David Douglas (1799–1834) whose first journey in 1823 took him to the east coast of America, through New York and Pennsylvania then up to Canada, followed the next year by a trip to the west coast of America. He is most famous for his introductions of many forms of conifer, including the Douglas fir, *Pseudotsuga menziesii* syn *P douglassii*, and was almost single-handedly responsible for the fashion for growing fir trees that developed over the following decades and lasted through the Victorian and Edwardian eras.

Mulberry, Morus nigra

Commercial nurseries

During the 18th century the number of nurseries in London, the centre of the plant trade, increased from 15 to 200. Improved growing and cultivation techniques included providing heat for tender specimens using open fires fuelled by wood or charcoal. New plants became increasingly available, in larger numbers and to a wider population. Together with seeds and the catalogues in which they were advertised, plants were transported along the country's growing network of roads and canals. As understanding about seed production and the 'sexual' propagation of plants grew, people began to experiment to see if nature could be improved upon. One of the first attempts at developing better forms of flowers was Thomas Fairchild's crossing of the pinks *Dianthus caryophyllus* and *Dianthus barbatus* to produce what was referred to as 'Fairchild's mule'. In 1725, The Society of Gardeners and London Nurserymen was founded to bring order to the naming, identifying and recording of ornamental plants.

The importation of non-native plants, seeds, roots, tubers and bulbs depended on an effective and reliable transportation system. Long, hazardous sea journeys usually meant specimens were deprived of good cultivation conditions for months on end. Salt spray, lack of fresh water and light, damp conditions, scavenging vermin and a lack of horticultural knowledge on-board ship meant a massive proportion of collected

Sweet William or bearded pink, Dianthus barbatus, *from* William Curtis's Botanical Magazine, *1793*

Opposite: The Belladonna lily, Amaryllis belladonna, *introduced to Britain from South Africa in 1712*

59

material was lost during transit. Since the 17th century, when commercial plant hunting expeditions began, botanists and gardeners had attempted to find ways to improve this survival rate. These included wrapping roots in moss and earth and storing seed in sand, paper or even individual wax balls. When seedsman John Ellis published *Directions for Bringing over Seeds and Plants from the East Indies and other Distant Countries in a state of Vegetation in 1770*, he stated '…yet it is certain that scarcely one in fifty [plants] ever comes to anything, except a few varieties of annual plants.' The title of his first chapter gives an indication of the regularity with which merchant ships transported plants and seeds:

> *Directions for Captains of Ships, Sea Surgeons*
> *and other curious persons who collect Seeds and*
> *Plants in distant Countries, in what manner to*
> *preserve them fit for vegetation.*

By the 18th century, with sea journeys longer than ever, it became imperative to find a way of ensuring that plant material arrived in Britain in a viable condition. Various methods of enclosing plants in glass or wooden cases were tried but it was not until the very end of the Georgian period, in the early 1830s, that a chance observation by Dr Nathaniel Bagshaw Ward (1791–1868) led to the design of the Wardian Case. His sealed, glass-roofed boxes created microclimates where plants were rooted in soil and had sufficient moisture and light for photosynthesis to take place. From then on, the survival rate of transported plants increased dramatically and allowed a viable commercial trading system to begin.

Commercial nurseries had been supplying plants to garden and landscape designers as well as to the general public well before this development. One of the earliest and most influential was the Brompton Park Nursery, owned by George London (1681–1714) and Henry Wise (1653–1738). Their work of supplying plants and designing gardens was heavily influenced by formal French gardens and they sold quantities of topiary, potted citrus fruits and yew, holly and box hedging. Unfortunately the nursery did not survive the demise of formal gardens as the 18th century progressed.

Loddiges nursery was originally established in about 1756, in what was then the rural area of Hackney, London, by German nurseryman John Busch. Like Philip Miller at the Chelsea Physic Garden, Busch was one of the recipients of 'Bartram's Boxes' of seeds from Philadelphia. This enabled him to sell rare and much-sought-after plants at great profit. A fellow German, Joachim Conrad Loddiges, took over the established business in 1771 and later formed a partnership with his son, George. Loddiges is thought to have been the first nursery to grow *Rhododendron ponticum*, which was popular in the early 19th

century but has since become an environmental thug, swamping small native plants in British woodlands. The nursery was also involved in the development of the Wardian Case and in the mid 1820s a vast stove-house was built to house orchids and other tropical plants. Loddiges was in fact the first nursery to successfully grow epiphytic orchids (ones that grow on other plants) and by 1830, at the end of the Georgian period, the nursery was the largest in Europe and employed freelance collectors to bring new seeds and plants for commercial propagation.

The Veitch Nursery was originally founded in 1802 by John Veitch (1752–1839) in Killerton, Devon, but expanded when his son James (1792–1863) joined the company. It moved to Exeter in 1832, then took over The Royal Exotic Nurseries in the King's Road Chelsea, from where grandson James (1815–69) established the nursery's London base. From the early days the Veitch's employed their own plant hunters, commissioning 22 men over a period of 65 years. The heyday of the Veitch nursery, however, was in the Victorian and Edwardian periods, when great names like Thomas and William Lobb and Ernest 'Chinese' Wilson collected for the nursery from all over the world. The RHS Veitch Memorial Medal, awarded to those who have made outstanding contributions to horticulture, demonstrates how influential the family have been to British horticulture.

As tastes migrated away from the formal towards landscape gardens, demand grew for a completely different nursery stock. Requests for trained and topiarised evergreens supplied by the likes of the Brompton Nursery were replaced by a new market for trees with a natural shape . At the peak of the Landscape Movement, deciduous and evergreen trees were planted in large groups or 'plantations' that combined indigenous trees with non-natives. Newly introduced North American specimens were popular, including conifers such as red cedar, *Juniperus virginiana*, and the balsam fir *Abies balsamea*, and a fashion for creating 'American' gardens developed.

Capability Brown planted hundreds of thousands of trees during his career. He used them for their mass effect, as in the large groups used at Blenheim Palace in Oxfordshire, rather than for the beauty of any individual specimen. His choice was influenced by the effect of light and shade on leaf colour and he planted both native and introduced species. He gained a reputation for heavily over planting, because he operated a 'sacrificial' system whereby some young trees were used to protect others as they matured, and were removed at a later date. This technique is still practised today.

It was also popular to plant flowering shrubs *en masse,* or to use them as under-planting within the plantations and the fashion for separating evergreen and deciduous shrubs relaxed as the 18th century progressed. Shrubs were used to create 'wilderness' planting, with specimens such as lilac, philadelphus, ceanothus and forms of viburnum bordering woodland paths and walks, with jasmine, briar rose, violets, primroses and daffodils planted through and beneath the woody plants.

Repton's softening of Capability Brown's more extreme style of landscape gardening saw the resurgence of interest in the flower garden. Beds and borders were created around the terrace and in the lawn near the house and he planted roses in abundance: in rose gardens, mixed borders, up poles, along

Mountain Laurel, Kalmia latifolia, *from Curtis's* Botanical Magazine, *1796*

ropes and scrambling through trees. His island beds were planted with a mixture of flowering shrubs, herbaceous plants and bulbs, and edged with delicate, 'basket-weave' wire structures.

For the first time in history, the character of British gardens was almost entirely dictated by 'soft' rather than 'hard' landscaping: by plants and earth, rather than architecture. Roman, medieval and Tudor gardens had, in one way or another, all responded to buildings and enclosures, and the Victorian period would see a return to a love of Italianate architecture, which would be developed and refined throughout the Edwardian era. The great landscape gardens of the 18th century saw Britain flexing her horticultural muscles in preparation for becoming an international influence in garden making as, for the first time, British styles and designs were being copied abroad. European formality no longer dictated the appearance of this nation's landscapes, and it could be argued that the English Landscape Garden became Britain's greatest artistic export.

The view from Kenwood House today could almost have been planned to frame the towers of modern London

create rose swags

Plant a rose in a generous hole at the base of each post, and add large amounts of organic matter to the soil. Modern roses like 'Bantry Bay, 'Golden Showers' or 'Etude' will provide a long flowering season, but if you want to use 18th-century plants try *Rosa alba* 'Maiden's Blush' or *Rosa eglanteria* syn *rubiginosa*.

Tie the rose so that it bends around the post – avoid any upright growth to encourage better flowering. You will need to continue tying it in throughout the growing season. Once the rose has reached the top of the post, over the next season or two, it can be tied onto the rope swag.

Humphry Repton often planted roses in his gardens and grew ramblers up posts and along rope swags. These structures look attractive behind rose beds or flower borders, or along paths. 'Rustic' posts will work best for this project, for example untreated larch poles with the bark still in place. Use posts 2.4m (8 feet) high and drive them roughly 600mm (2 feet) into the ground.

Use natural ropes to create the 'swags'; try a ship's chandler or boat yard if you have difficulty finding these. Secure the rope to the top of each post; one method is to drill hole through the tops of the posts and feed the rope through, securing the ends with nails.

The following lists of plants, while not exhaustive, give an indication of plants that were available in Georgian Britain. Only those of interest to the gardener have been included so crops and 'non-ornamental' plants are excluded. All the plants listed are available either as seed, container-grown plants or as bare-rooted trees and shrubs. You might find that some of the plants are not readily available in their Georgian forms. It is crucial then to decide whether your planting must be authentic or whether it is to be 'in the style of' Georgian planting, in which case you will have a wider palette to select from and will find the plants easier to obtain.

Many cultivated forms of plants are only available as container-grown specimens because they are often propagated vegetatively, for example as cuttings or by layering. However, most annuals and many British wild flowers, native or naturalised, are rarely sold in garden centres as established plants because they are short-lived and uneconomical to grow on a commercial scale. You will have to grow such plants from seed obtained from specialist suppliers.

Please remember that under the Wildlife and Countryside Act it is illegal uproot any wild plant and to take material from protected species. All the plants listed in this book are available from legitimate sources.

Chinese wisteria, Wisteria sinensis, *introduced in 1816*

BOTANICAL NAME	COMMON NAME	PLANTS	SEED
Tender/half hardy			
Agave americana	American aloe	🪴 🪴	◆
Aloe variegata	Partridge breast aloe	🪴	◆
Amaryllis belladonna	Belladonna lily	🪴	◆
Arabis alpina subsp *caucasica*	Alpine rock cress		◆
Astelia nervosa	Bush flax	🪴	◆
Aubrieta deltoidea	Aubretia	🪴	◆
Banksia integrifolia	Coast banksia	🪴	◆
Banksia serrata	Saw banksia	🪴	◆
Begonia grandis subsp *evansiana*	Beefsteak plant	🪴	◆
Calceolaria corymbosa		🪴	◆
Calceolaria integrifolia	Slipperwort	🪴	◆
Citrus reticulate	Mandarin, orange, tangerine, clementine, satsuma	🪴	◆
Cosmos bipinnatus	Cosmos	Cultivars available	◆
Dahlia coccinea	Scarlet dahlia	🪴	◆
Dahlia pinnata		Cultivars available	◆
Ficus elastica	India rubber tree	🪴	◆
Fuchsia triphylla		🪴	◆
Gaillardia aristata	Blanket flower	🪴	◆ ◆
Gardenia jasminoides	Cape jasmine	🪴	◆
Hedychium gardnerianum	Kahili ginger	🪴 🪴	◆
Heliotropium arborescens	Common heliotrope	🪴	◆
Musa acuminate	Commercial banana	🪴	◆
Pelargonium capitatum	Rose-scented geranium	🪴	◆
Pelargonium fulgidum	Pelargonium	🪴	◆

BOTANICAL NAME	COMMON NAME	PLANTS	SEED
Pelargonium inquinans		🪴	◆
Pelargonium peltatum	Ivy-leaved geranium	🪴	◆
Pelargonium zonale	Horseshoe geranium	🪴	◆
Strelitzia reginae	Bird of paradise	🪴	◆ ◆
Tagetes minuta	Mexican marigold	Cultivars available	◆

Bulbs

BOTANICAL NAME	COMMON NAME	PLANTS	SEED
Allium cernuum	Nodding onion	🪴 🪴	◆ ◆
Anemone virginiana	Three-leaved windflower	🪴	◆
Camassia quamash	Common camassia	🪴	◆
Cyclamen purpurascens	Purple cyclamen	🪴	◆
Cyclamen repandum	Wavy cyclamen	🪴	◆
Erythronium grandiflorum	Curly lily	🪴	◆
Eucomis autumnalis	Autumn pineapple lily	🪴	◆
Eucomis comosa		🪴	◆
Eucomis regia	King's flower	🪴	◆
Gladiolus tristis	Evening flower	🪴	◆
Hepatica nobilis	Liverleaf	🪴 🪴	◆
Hyacinthus orientalis	Common hyacinth	🪴	◆
Iris latifolia	English iris	🪴	◆
Iris persica	Persian iris	🪴	◆
Iris pumila	Crimean iris	🪴	◆
Lilium lancifolium	Tiger lily	🪴	◆
Lilium superbum	Turk's cap lily	🪴	◆
Narcissus jonquilla	Jonquil	🪴	◆

BOTANICAL NAME	COMMON NAME	PLANTS	SEED
Narcissus minor	Lesser daffodil		
Narcissus poeticus	Pheasant's eye		
Narcissus pseudonarcissus	Wild daffodil		
Narcissus x odorus	Campernelle		
Ornithogalum longibracteatum	False sea onion		
Ornithogalum thyrsoides	Chincherinchee		
Puschkinia scilloides	Striped squill		
Trillium erectum	Birthroot		

Hardy perennials and annuals

Achillea filipendulina	Fern-leaf yarrow		
Aconitum japonicum	Japonese monkshood		
Aconitum x cammarum	Purple wolf's bane	Cultivars available	
Actaea cimicifuga			
Actaea racemosa	Black snakeroot		
Anchusa azurea	Garden anchusa		
Antirrhinum majus	Greater snapdragon		
Aster novi-belgii	Michaelmas daisy		
Bergenia cordifolia			
Bergenia crassifolia	Elephant ears		
Brunnera macrophylla	Siberian bugloss		
Caltha palustris 'Flore Pleno'	Double marsh marigold		
Campanula bononiensis			
Campanula carpatica	American harebell		
Campanula cenisia			

BOTANICAL NAME	COMMON NAME	PLANTS	SEED
Campanula latiloba	Great bellflower	🪴	◆
Campanula punctata	Long-flowered harebell	🪴 🪴	◆
Campanula versicolor		🪴	◆
Cephalaria gigantea	Giant scabious	🪴 🪴	◆
Chelone glabra	Balmony	🪴 🪴	◆
Chelone oblique	Twisted shell flower	🪴 🪴	◆
Coreopsis lanceolata	Tickseed	🪴	◆ ◆
Delphinium grandiflorum	Bouquet larkspur	🪴	◆
Dianthus alpinus	Alpine pink	🪴	◆
Dianthus superbus	Fringed pink	🪴	◆
Dicentra cucullaria	Dutchman's breeches	🪴 🪴	◆
Dicentra formosa	Common bleeding heart	🪴 🪴	◆
Dicentra spectabilis	Bleeding heart	🪴 🪴	◆
Digitalis lanata	Grecian foxglove	🪴 🪴	◆
Digitalis parviflora		🪴 🪴	◆
Eryngium bourgatii		🪴 🪴	◆
Eryngium giganteum	Miss Willmott's ghost	🪴 🪴	◆
Eschscholzia californica	California poppy	🪴	◆ ◆
Euphorbia polychroma	Many-coloured spurge	🪴 🪴	◆
Euphorbia rigida		🪴 🪴	◆
Galega orientalis	Goat's rue	🪴	◆
Gentiana andrewsii	Bottle gentian	🪴	◆
Geranium endressii	Endres's cranesbill	🪴 🪴	◆
Geranium ibericum	Caucasian cranesbill	🪴	◆
Geranium maculatum	Alum bloom	🪴	◆

BOTANICAL NAME	COMMON NAME	PLANTS	SEED
Geranium pratense	Meadow cranesbill		
Geranium wallichianum			
Gypsophila paniculata	Baby's breath		
Helenium autumnale	Autumn helen flower		
Helleborus purpurascens	Purple-flowered Christmas rose		
Hosta lancifolia	Narrow-leaved plantain lily		
Hosta plantaginea	August lily		
Hosta sieboldii			
Hosta ventricosa	Blue plantain lily		
Lobelia erinus cultivars			
Lupinus polyphyllus			
Macleaya cordata	Plume poppy		
Matthiola longipetala subsp *bicornis*	Night-scented stock		
Nepeta racemosa syn mussinii	Raceme catnip/Catmint		
Paeonia brownie	Western peony		
Paeonia lactiflora	Edible-rooted peony		
Penstemon barbatus	Bearded penstemon		
Phlox maculate	Meadow phlox		
Phlox paniculata	Perennial phlox		
Pulsatilla vulgaris	Pasqueflower		
Ranunculus aconitifolius	Aconite buttercup		
Reseda odorata	Mignonette		
Rudbeckia hirta	Black-eyed Susan		
Scabiosa caucasica	Caucasian scabious		
Sedum populifolium			

Perennial phlox, Phlox paniculata, *introduced in 1730 from North America*

BOTANICAL NAME	COMMON NAME	PLANTS	SEED
Stachys byzantina syn *lanata*	Lambs' ears		
Verbascum phlomoides	Woolly mullein		
Verbascum phoeniceum	Purple mullein		
Verbena bonariensis	Argentinean vervain		
Verbena peruviana			
Veronica exaltata	Veronica		
Veronica gentianoides	Gentian speedwell		
Veronica spicata subsp *Incana*	Silver speedwell		
Vinca major	Greater periwinkle		
Viola odorata var *flore-pleno*	Double violet		
Zantedeschia aethiopica	Arum lily		

Shrubs

Aucuba japonica 'Variegata'	Spotted laurel		
Buddleja globosa	Orange ball tree		
Buxus balearica	Balearic box		
Callistemon citrinus	Bottlebrush flower		
Callistemon salignus	Pink tips		
Camellia japonica	Camellia	Cultivars available	
Ceanothus americanus	Indian tea		
Chaenomeles speciosa	Japanese quince		
Chimonanthus praecox	Wintersweet		
Cistus ladanifer	Common gum cistus		
Cistus laurifolius	Laurel-leaved rock rose		
Colutea orientalis	Red-flowered bladder senna		

BOTANICAL NAME	COMMON NAME	PLANTS	SEED
Cornus alba	Red-barked dogwood		
Cornus florida	Flowering dogwood		
Cotoneaster frigidus	Tree cotoneaster		
Cytisus scoparius	Common broom		
Daphne odora	Japan daphne		
Drimys winteri	Winter's bark		
Erythrina crista-galli	Christ's tears		
Erythrina herbacea	Cardinal spear		
Euonymus atropurpureus	Burning bush		
Euonymus japonicus	Evergreen spindle		
Fuchsia coccinea			
Fuchsia magellanica	Lady's teardrops		
Gaultheria procumbens	Checkerberry		
Grevillea rosmarinifolia	Rosemary grevillea		
Hippophae rhamnoides	Sea buckthorn		
Hydrangea arborescens	North american wild hydrangea		
Hydrangea quercifolia	Oak-leaved hydrangea		
Hypericum androsaemum	Tutsan		
Ilex glabra	Appalachian tea tree		
Ilex opaca	American holly		
Juniperus Sabina	Savin		
Kalmia angustifolia	Sheep laurel		
Kalmia latifolia	Mountain laurel/Calico bush		
Kalmia polifolia	Bog laurel		
Leptospermum lanigerum	Australian tea tree		

BOTANICAL NAME	COMMON NAME	PLANTS	SEED
Leptospermum polygalifolium		🪴	◆
Leptospermum scoparium	Tea tree	🪴	◆
Ligustrum lucidum	Chinese privet	🪴	◆
Ligustrum vulgare	Wild privet	🪴	◆
Lupinus arboreus	Tree lupin	🪴 🪴	◆
Mahonia aquifolium	Oregon grape	🪴	◆
Olearia paniculata	Daisy bush	🪴	◆
Osmanthus fragrans	Fragrant olive	🪴	◆
Paeonia suffruticosa	Moutan	🪴	◆
Philadelphus coronaries	Common mock orange	🪴	◆
Pieris floribunda	Fetterbush	🪴	◆
Pittosporum revolutum	Yellow-flowered brisbane laurel	🪴	◆
Pittosporum tenuifolium	New zealand pittosporum	🪴 🪴	◆
Pittosporum tobira	Japanese pittosporum	🪴 🪴	◆
Pittosporum undulatum	Cheesewood	🪴	◆
Pittosporum viridiflorum	Cape pittosporum	🪴	◆
Rhodendron viscosum	Swamp azalea	🪴	◆
Rhododendron arboretum		🪴	◆
Rhododendron canescens		🪴	◆
Rhododendron ferrugineum	Alpenrose	🪴	◆
Rhododendron luteum	Yellow azalea	🪴	◆
Rhododendron maximum	American rosebay	🪴	◆
Rhododendron periclymenoides	Pinxter flower	🪴	◆
Ribes sanguineum	Flowering currant	🪴	◆
Rosa alba 'Maiden's Blush'	Rose 'Maiden's Blush'	🪴	◆

BOTANICAL NAME	COMMON NAME	PLANTS	SEED
Rosa acicularis	Arctic rose		
Rosa eglanteria syn rubiginosa	Eglantine		
Rosa x centifolia	Cabbage rose		
Rosa x damascena var semperflorens	Autumn damask rose		
Ruscus aculeatus	Butcher's broom		
Sambucus nigra laciniata	Cut-leaved elder		
Sambucus racemosa	Red-berried elder		
Sophora tetraptera	Kowhai		
Spartium junceum	Spanish broom		
Spiraca salicifolia	Bridewort		
Tamarix gallica	Common tamarisk		
Viburnum opulus	Guelder rose		

Climbers

Clematis alpine	Austrian clematis		
Clematis montana	Mountain clematis		
Clematis orientalis	Oriental clematis		
Lathyrus nervosus	Lord Anson's blue pea		
Lonicera etrusca	Etruscan honeysuckle		
Lonicera implexa	Minorca honeysuckle		
Lonicera x americana	American woodbine		
Rosa banksiae	Double white banksian rose		
Wisteria floribunda	Japanese wisteria		
Wisteria frutescens	American kidney bean tree		
Wisteria sinensis	Chinese wisteria		

Maidenhair tree, Ginkgo biloba, introduced from China in 1750

BOTANICAL NAME	COMMON NAME	PLANTS	SEED
Trees			
Abies grandis	Grand fir	●	●
Acer platanoides	Norway maple	●	●
Acer rubrum	Red maple	● ●	●
Acer saccharinum	Silver maple	●	●
Ailanthus altissima	Tree of heaven	●	●
Araucaria araucana	Monkey puzzle	● ●	●
Arbutus andrachne	Grecian strawberry tree	●	●
Betula nigra	Black birch	●	●
Betula papyrifera	Paper birch	●	●
Betula pendula 'Laciniata'	Swedish birch	● ●	●
Carpinus betulus	Common hornbeam	● ●	●
Catalpa bignonioides	Indian bean tree	● ●	●
Chamaecyparis thyoides	White cypress	Cultivars available	●
Dicksonia antarctica	Woolly tree fern	● ●	●
Fagus grandifolia	American beech	●	●
Fagus sylvatica Atropurpurea group	Copper beech	● ●	●
Fraxinus americana	American ash	●	●
Fraxinus excelsior	Common ash	●	●
Fraxinus ornus	Manna ash	●	●
Ginkgo biloba	Maidenhair tree	● ●	● ●
Halesia Carolina	Opossum wood	● ●	●
Koelreuteria paniculata	Pride of India/Golden rain tree	● ●	● ●
Magnolia acuminata	Cucumber tree	●	●
Magnolia fraseri		●	●

Further reading

Batey, Mavis *Regency Gardens*. Princes Risborough: Shire, 1995

Batey, Mavis and Lambert, David *The English Garden Tour*. London: John Murray, 1990

Campbell-Culver, Maggie *The Origin of Plants*, London: Headline Book Publishing, 2001

Chambers, Douglas D C *The Planters of the English Landscape Garden*. Yale: Yale University Press, 1993

Clifford, Joan *Capability Brown, an illustrated life of Lancelot Brown*, 1716–1783. Princes Risborough: Shire, 1983

Cobbett, William *The English Gardener*. London: Bloomsbury gardening classics. New edn, 1998

Fearnley-Whittingstall, Jane *The Garden, An English Love Affair*. London: Weidenfeld & Nicholson, 2003

Fleming, Laurence and Gore, Alan *The English Garden*. London: Spring Books, 1988

Harvey, John *Restoring Period Gardens: From the Middle Ages to Georgian Times*. Princes Risborough: Shire, 1993

Hobhouse, Penelope *Plants in Garden History* London: Pavilion, 1997

Jackson, Hazelle *Shell Houses and Grottoes*. Princes Risborough: Shire, 2001

Jacques, David *Georgian Gardens: The Reign of Nature*. London: Batsford, 1983

Laird, Mark *The Flowering of the Landscape Garden: English Pleasure Grounds, 1720–1800*. University of Pennsylvania Press, 1999

Longstaffe-Gowan, Todd *The London Town Garden 1700–1840*. Yale: Yale University Press, 2001

le Rougetel, Hazel *The Chelsea Gardener Philip Miller 1691–1771*. London: Natural History Museum Publications, 1990

Royal Horticultural Society *RHS A-Z Encyclopaedia of Garden Plants (Vols I & II)*, London: Dorling Kindersley, 2003

Stone, Jean *The Rustic Garden*. London: Batsford, 1992

Symes, Michael *A Glossary of Garden History*. Princes Risborough: Shire, 2000

The RHS Plant Finder
Published annually by the Royal Horticultural Society, the *Plant Finder* lists more than 65,000 plants available from 800 nurseries as well as contact details, maps and opening hours for all the nurseries listed. There is also an online version of the *Plant Finder* on the RHS website: www.rhs.org.uk

The Seed Search
Now in its 5th edition, *The Seed Search* lists over 40,000 seeds available from 500 seed suppliers, with details of where to find them. It also includes 9,000 vegetable cultivars. Compiled and edited by Karen Platt, and online: www.seedsearch.demon.co.uk

Fern-leaf yarrow, Achillea filipendulina, *arrived in Britain from the Caucasus in 1803*

Useful organisations and societies

The Museum of Garden History
The Museum of Garden History exists to enhance understanding and appreciation of the history and development of gardens and gardening in the U.K., and was the world's first museum dedicated to this subject. Its attractions include a recreated17th-century knot garden with historically authentic planting and collections of tools and gardening ephemera, as well as a well-stocked library.
www.museumgardenhistory.org

The Garden History Society
The Garden History Society aims to promote the study of the history of gardening, landscape gardens and horticulture, and to promote the protection and conservation of historic parks, gardens and designed landscapes and advise on their restoration. The Society runs a series of lectures, tours and events throughout the year.
www.gardenhistorysociety.org

The Royal Horticultural Society
The RHS is the world's leading horticultural organisation and the UK's leading gardening charity dedicated to advancing horticulture and promoting good gardening. It offers free horticultural advice and a seed service for its members and has plant centres at its four flagship gardens.
www.rhs.org.uk

The National Council for the Conservation of Plants and Gardens
The NCCPG seeks to conserve, document, promote and make available Britain and Ireland's garden plants for the benefit of horticulture, education and science. Its National Plant Collection scheme has 630 National Collections held in trust by private owners, specialist growers, arboreta, colleges, universities and botanic gardens.
www.nccpg.com

The Hardy Plant Society
With over 40 local groups in the UK, the Hardy Plant Society encourages interest in growing hardy perennial plants and provides members with information on both familiar and rarer perennial plants, how to grow them and where to find them. Its annual seed list is available for members to use and contribute to.
www.hardy-plant.org.uk

The Henry Doubleday Research Association
HDRA is a registered charity, and Europe's largest organic membership organisation. It is dedicated to researching and promoting organic gardening, farming and food. The HDRA's Heritage Seed Library saves hundreds of old and unusual vegetable varieties for posterity, also distributing them to its members. The HDRA currently manages the kitchen garden at Audley End, Essex, for English Heritage and runs Yalding Organic Gardens (see Places to visit).
www.hdra.org.uk

Centre for Organic Seed Information
Funded by DEFRA and run by the National Institute of Agricultural Botany and the Soil Association, the Centre for Organic Seed Information is a 'one-stop shop' for sourcing certified-organic seed from listed suppliers. It covers fruits, vegetables, grasses, herbs and ornamental plants among others.
www.cosi.org.uk

Local gardens trust and national plant societies
Almost all counties and regions of the UK have their own gardens trusts and most genera of plants have a national society. Your local groups may have fundraising plant sales or a members' seed list that you could join.

Places to visit

Ashridge
Ringshall
Berkhamsted
Hertfordshire HP4 1NS
Tel: 01442 851227
E-mail: ashridge@nationaltrust.org.uk
www.nationaltrust.org.uk

Bath Georgian Garden
The Gravel Walk
Bath
Tel: 01225 477752
E mail:
costume_enquiries@bathnes.gov.uk
www.bathnes.gov.uk

Blenheim Palace
Woodstock
Oxfordshire OX20 1PX
Tel: 08700 602080
E-mail:
operations@blenheimpalace.co.uk
www.blenheimpalace.com

Blickling Hall
Blicklling
Norwich
Norfolk NR11 6NF
Tel: 01263 738030
E-mail: blickling@nationaltrust.org.uk
www.nationaltrust.org.uk

Chiswick House
Burlington Lane
Chiswick
London W4 2RP
Tel: 020 8995 0508
www.english-heritage.org.uk

Claremont Landscape Garden
Portsmouth Road
Esher
Surrey KT10 9JG
Tel: 01372 467806
E-mail: claremont@nationaltrust.org.uk
www.nationaltrust.org.uk

Cliveden
Taplow
Maidenhead
Buckinghamshire SI6 0JA
Tel: 01628 605069
E-mail: cliveden@nationaltrust.org.uk
www.nationaltrust.org.uk

Dyrham Park
Chippenham
Gloucestershire SN14 8ER
Tel: 0117 937 2501
E-mail: dyrhampark@nationaltrust.org.uk
www.nationaltrust.org.uk

Eaton Hall
Eccleston
Chester
Cheshire CH4 9FT
Tel: 01244 684400
www.eeo.co.uk/grosvenor_estate/eaton
g_ardens.asp

Gibside
Rowlands Gill
Burnopfield
Gateshead
Newcastle NE16 6BG
Tel: 01207 541820
E-mail: gibside@nationaltrust.org.uk
www.nationaltrust.org.uk

Hagley Hall
Stourbridge
West Midlands DY9 9LG
Tel: 01562 882408
E-mail: contact@hagleyhall.info
www.hagleyhall.info

Harewood House
Harewood
Leeds
West Yorkshire LS17 9LQ
Tel: 0113 218 1010
E-mail: info@harewood.org
www.harewood.org

Holkham Hall
Wells-next-the-Sea
Norfolk NR23 1AB
Tel: 01328 710227
E-mail: enquiries@holkham.co.uk
www.holkhamgardens.com

Kedleston Hall
Derby
Derbyshire DE22 5JH
Tel: 01332 842191
E-mail:
kedlestonhall@nationaltrust.org.uk
www.nationaltrust.org.uk

Kensington Gardens
Park Lane
London W2
Tel: 020 7298 2000
E-mail: hq@royalparks.gsi.gov.uk
www.royalparks.gov.uk

Kenwood House
Kenwood
London
Tel:
E-mail: customers@english-
heritage.org.uk
www.english-heritage.org.uk

The Leasowes
Mucklow Hill
Halesowen
Warwickshire
Tel: 01384 814642
www.gardenvisit.com/g/leas.htm

Marble Hill Hall
Twickenham
Middlesex
Tel:
E-mail:
www.english-heritage.org.uk

Places to visit

Melbourne Hall Gardens
Church Square
Melbourne
Derbyshire DE73 1EN
Tel: 01332 862502
www.melbournehall.com

Minterne
Minterne Magna
Cerne Abbas
Dorset DT2 7AU
Tel: 01300 341370
www.aboutbritain.dom/minternegardens.com

Mount Edgcumbe House
Cremyll
Torpoint
Cornwall PL10 1HZ
Tel: 01752 822236
E-mail: mt.edgcumbe@plymouth.gov.uk
www.mountedgcumbe.gov.uk

Painshill Landscape Garden
Portsmouth Road
Cobham
Surrey KT11 1JE
Tel: 01932 868113
E-mail: info@painshill.co.uk
www.painshill.co.uk

Petworth House
Petworth
West Sussex GU28 0AE
Tel: 01798 342207
E-mail: petworth@nationaltrust.org.uk
www.nationaltrust.org.uk

Pope's Villa
19 Cross Deep
Twickenham
Middlesex TW1 4QG
Tel: 020 8892 2002
www.twickenham-museum.org.uk
(open by appointment only)

Rousham House
Steeple Aston
Bicester
Oxfordshire
OX25 4QX
Tel: 01869 347110
www.rousham.org

Scotney Castle
Lamberhurst
Tunbridge Wells
Kent TN3 8JN
Tel: 01892 891081
E-mail:
scotneycastle@nationaltrust.org.uk
www.nationaltrust.org.uk

Sheringham Park
Upper Sheringham
Norfolk NR26 8TB
Tel: 01263 823778
E-mail:
sheringhampark@nationaltrust.org.uk
www.nationaltrust.org.uk

Shugborough
Great Haywood
Milford
Staffordshire ST17 0XB
Tel: 01889 881388
www.nationaltrust.org.uk

Squerryes Court
Westerham
Kent TN16 1SJ
Tel: 01959 562345
E-mail: enquiries@squerryes.co.uk
www.squerryes.co.uk

Stourhead
Stourton
Warminster
Wiltshire BA12 6QD
Tel: 01747 841152
E-mail: stourhead@nationaltrust.org.uk
www.nationaltrust.org.uk

Stowe Landscape Gardens
Buckingham
Buckinghamshire MK18 5EH
Tel: 01280 822850
E-mail:
stowegarden@nationaltrust.org.uk
www.nationaltrust.org.uk

Syon Park
Brentford
Middlesex TW8 8JF
Tel: 010 8560 0881
E-mail: info@syonpark.co.uk
www.syonpark.co.uk

Wentworth Castle
Lowe Lane
Stainborough
Barnsley
South Yorkshire S75 3ET
Tel: 01226 731269
E-mail: m.stannard@northernac.uk
www.wentworthcastle.org

Westonbirt Arboretum
Tetbury
Gloucestershire GL8 8QS
Tel: 01666 880220
www.westonbirtarboretum.com

Wilton House
Wilton
Salisbury
Wiltshire SP2 0BJ
Tel: 01722 746720
E-mail: tourism@wiltonhouse.com
www.wiltonhouse.co.uk

Wrest Park
Silsoe
Bedfordshire MK45 4HS
Tel: 01525 860152
E-mail: customers@english-heritage.org.uk
www.english-heritage.org.uk

Acknowledgements and picture credits

English Heritage and the Museum of Garden History would like to thank the many individuals who contributed to this volume, in particular Rowan Blaik for technical editing, James O Davies for photography and Michael Bidnell at The Georgian Group, as well as colleagues at the National Monuments Record for picture research. Thanks to Royal Botanic Gardens Kew and Bath Georgian Garden for allowing access to the gardens for photography and to Livvy Gullen for further research.

The author would like to acknowledge the invaluable assistance of Jane Wilson, Fiona Hope and Philip Norman at the Museum of Garden History.

Unless stated otherwise images are © English Heritage. All English Heritage photographs taken by James O Davies, except for Jonathan Bailey: 17; Nigel Corrie: 4, bc; John Critchley: 2; Paul Highnam: 65; Pat Payne: 18l, 23, 25; Jeremy Richards: 16. Original artwork by Judith Dobie.

Other illustrations reproduced by permission of:
Jacques Amand: 58; The Art Archive: 12t, 48; Bridgeman Art Library: 6, 15, 26 (The Stapleton Collection), 27, 32 (Victoria & Albert Museum) 34 & 35 (The Stapleton Collection), 45, 50 (Christie's), 51; Roger Cove, Silsoe Research Institute: 18r, 21b; The Georgian Group: 8, 29, 37, 44; Mary Evans Picture Library: 22, 56, 59, 64, 83; Museum of Garden History: 12b, 13, 41t, 46t, 62; National Portrait Gallery: 46b (D12900).

Every effort has been made to trace copyright holders and we apologise in advance for any unintentional omissions or errors, which we would be pleased to correct in any subsequent edition of the book.

About the author

Anne Jennings is a freelance garden designer, consultant and writer, and Head of Horticulture at the Museum of Garden History. She is the co-author of *Knot Gardens and Parterres*, published by Barn Elms, and writes for a variety of gardening magazines.

Other titles in this series

Medieval Gardens

Edwardian Gardens